Contents

A Few Initial Questions

Billions of living beings exist on earth. The trees, grasses in the prairies, and masses of algae form the "green carpet" of the earth. Sea urchins and jellyfish, crabs and octopuses, fishes and dolphins dwell in the seas. On the continents live rabbits, foxes, antelopes, lions, and also snakes. Above the earth fly seagulls, eagles, and a multitude of sparrows, not counting the myriad insects that gather pollen from flowers.

And in the middle of this swarming of different creatures evolved a species in many ways different from others: the human species—ours.

Where do we come from? What distinguishes us from other living beings? In fact, what do we know about ourselves?

In this book we shall try to answer these questions by following the traces of our ancestors. We shall see how the first humans evolved and how their techniques and their living conditions improved. It is certainly a fascinating history, which goes back millions of years.

First, let us discuss some questions that often receive partly or completely incorrect answers.

Is the Human a Descendant of the Ape?

Considering present monkeys and apes and those that lived hundreds of thousands of years ago, the answer is emphatically: no.

Indeed, whether marmosets or chimpanzees, macaques or gorillas, monkeys and apes have unquestionably a family likeness with humans. They look much more like a human

PREHISTORY
FROM AUSTRALOPITHECUS
TO MAMMOTH HUNTERS

(Original French title:
*La Préhistoire des Australopithèques aux
Chasseurs de Mammouths*)

by
Jean-Jacques Barloy

Translated from the French by
Albert V. Carozzi and Marguerite Carozzi

First English language edition published in 1987 by Barron's Educational
Series, Inc.

© 1986 Hachette S.A., 79, boulevard Saint-Germain, 75006 Paris

The title of the French edition is *La Préhistoire des Australopithèques aux
Chasseurs de Mammouths.*

International Standard Book No. 0-8120-3835-5

BARRON'S

New York • London • Toronto • Sydney

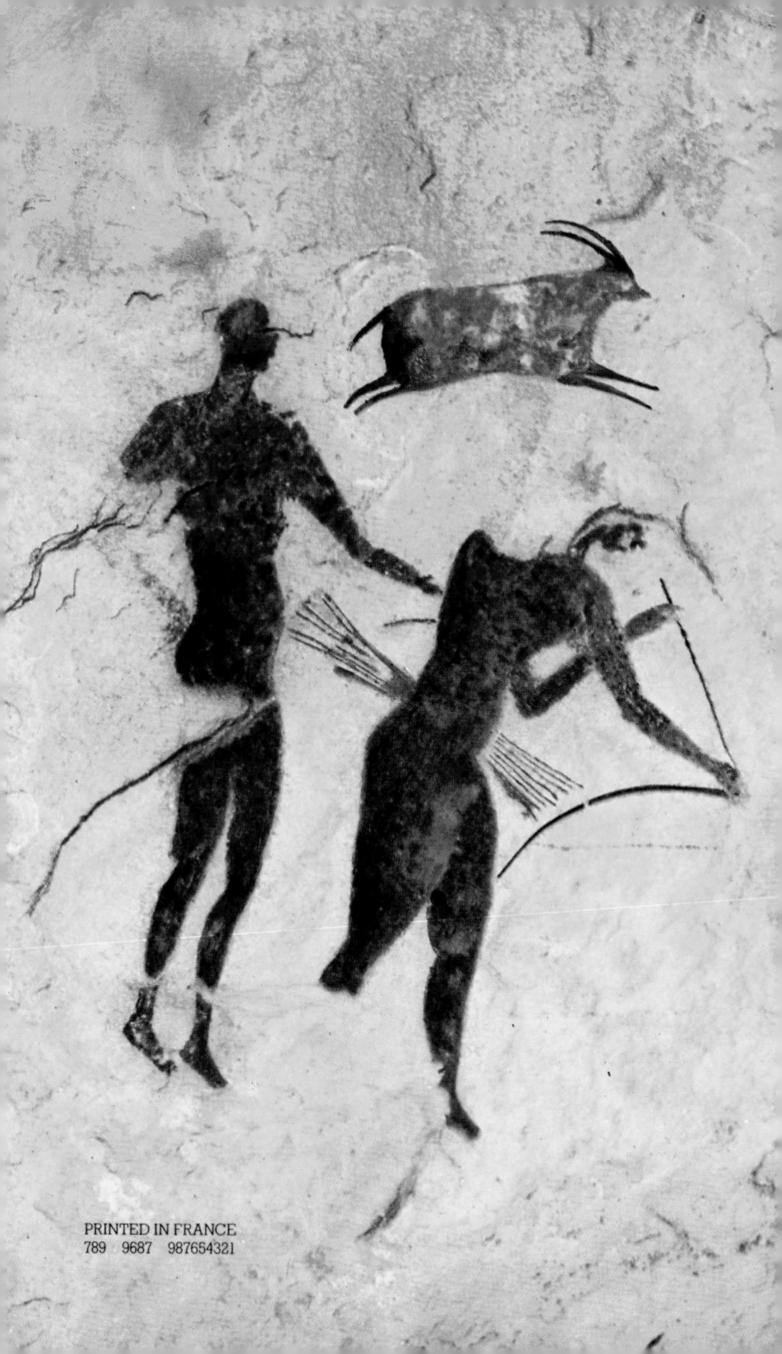

PRINTED IN FRANCE
789 9687 987654321

being than, for instance, a dog or a cow. Certainly, fundamental differences exist between us and monkeys and apes. In particular, they have proportionally longer arms and walk on all fours. Their intelligence, although superior to that of most other animals, nevertheless remains very rudimentary compared with ours. In fact, in that respect, an unbridgeable gap separates us.

The family likeness is nevertheless troublesome. Is there really no kinship between them and ourselves? There is. In the very remote past, the lineages of humans and of monkeys and apes had, as we shall see, common ancestors. Therefore, we do have some kind of monkeys or apes in our ancestry.

However, these lineages separated completely at least 5 to 8 million years ago. Therefore, present monkeys or apes are not our siblings and even less our parents. Let us say that we can consider them our cousins, many times removed.

An ax, a knife made from flint and then fastened to a wooden handle.

Did "Cavemen" Live in Caves?

The term "caveman" implies that the evolution of the human species was closely related to a particular type of habitat—as if our ancestors could not survive without hiding in caves. This is a very simplistic view of reality.

Unquestionably, when caves existed nearby, prehistoric people used them as shelters during harsh weather. Certainly, some caves were permanently inhabited. Indeed, troglodytes—populations living in caves—still exist today in some parts of the world (for example, in the southern part of Tunisia).

However, numerous human tribes lived in natural environments that almost lacked caves: forests, savannas, and steppes. We know today that our ancestors learned very early to construct artificial shelters, huts made of branches or of skins stretched between posts. Therefore, it is inappropriate to call our possible ancestors by the general name of "cavemen."

__Armed only with poles__ and pieces of rock, prehistoric hunters dared to attack the fearsome cave bear, a giant 2.5 meters (8 feet) high. It was a dangerous undertaking, but the meat and the fur of the animal made it worth taking some risks.

The objection may be raised: why were the most beautiful art works of prehistoric times found precisely in caves?

It may be assumed that the interiors of huts were also decorated, but since these fragile dwellings have disappeared, no traces are left. Furthermore, it is obvious that prehistoric artists wanted to make lasting works. Where else but in caves could they find solid walls sheltered from wind and rain?

Caves provide natural shelters that our ancestors knew how to use in regions where they could find them. However, they did not all live in caves.

Did Our Ancestors Fight Dinosaurs?

Some movies and cartoons show prehistoric people fighting giant reptiles like dinosaurs. These awesome battles are purely imaginary.

Indeed, our ancestors could never have encountered these monsters because the dinosaurs disappeared about 70 million years ago. Fossils of the first creatures resembling humans, the first hominids, are only some 4 million years old.

Nevertheless, our ancestors had to hunt or fight impressive animals now gone: the mammoth, the fearsome cave bear, and the no less dangerous cave lion, as well as other wild beasts.

These various questions having been answered, the trip into the past can begin.

At night, wild beasts wandered around huts. To frighten them away, these people used fire.

Toward the Dawn of Humankind

History began with the invention of writing about 5000 years ago. Prehistoric times (that is, the period "before history"), include the evolution of humans from their first appearance to that date. There is a tendency to stretch the length of prehistoric times. Indeed, this designation sometimes encompasses the immense span of time that preceded history since the appearance of life, or even the formation of the earth! This designation is inappropriate.

The history of the changes of our planet belongs to geology. That of the evolution of living things belongs to *paleontology*, a science that studies the remains of plants and animals that lived in the past. These remains—in particular bones of animals—are called fossils. Human paleontology (or paleoanthropology) is the branch that studies fossil human remains.

Archaeology is the science that pertains only to humans. It does not study their bones only but also their activities. Archaeologists study the traces left by people even before the beginning of writing: tools, weapons, jewelry, paintings, sculpture, the remains of dwellings—in summary, the ways of living and thinking of humankind.

First a geologic framework is necessary for the trip into the past.

In the swamps of the Paleozoic a first important step of evolution occurred: the exit from water. The first vertebrate that attempted this adventure was Ichthyostega, an amphibian already provided with lungs and legs but still with a fish-like tail.

Dinosaurs, giant reptiles of the Mesozoic, *included numerous species. Among them was Diplodocus, a peaceful herbivore in spite of its 30-meter (100-foot) length that, like the present hippopotamus, liked to live in water.*

The Major Stages of the History of the Earth

The earth was formed about 4.5 billion years ago. Life appeared on its surface 1 billion years later.

The Paleozoic began 570 million years ago. Living beings then became abundant in the seas. Soon some species began to leave the water to venture onto land. However, these animals returned to the sea or to lakes in order to reproduce. They led, so to speak, a double life, both terrestrial and aquatic, hence their name *amphibians,* derived from Greek roots. This is still the case today for frogs, toads, and other amphibians.

The Mesozoic began about 200 million years ago. It is called the age of reptiles. It was indeed the time when dinosaurs and other giant reptiles

Era	Period	Beginning
Quaternary	Holocene	0.01
	Pleistocene	2
Tertiary	Pliocene	5
	Miocene	25
	Oligocene	38
	Eocene	55
	Paleocene	65
Mesozoic	Cretaceous	144
	Jurassic	213
	Triassic	248
Paleozoic	Permian	286
	Carboniferous	360
	Devonian	408
	Silurian	438
	Ordovician	505
	Cambrian	590
Precambrian	Algonkian	2600
	Archean	3500
Formation of the earth		4600

ruled the earth.

These monsters, as we have seen, disappeared about 70 million years ago. This very approximative date corresponds to the beginning of the Cenozoic (Tertiary).

How does the Tertiary differ from the preceding era? Some of the major differences are great geologic events, such as the formation of the Alps and the opening of the North Atlantic. Furthermore, the mammals, which had appeared and developed alongside the dinosaurs, greatly expanded. Large mammals appeared. Thus, the origins of human beings, which are mammals, can be traced to the Tertiary. The first true hominids, which are beings related to humans and which walked on two legs, made their first appearance in the Quaternary.

Evolution Leading to the Human

Our evolution is known in a broad sense. For a long time, it was part of the evolution of all animals with a backbone, namely, *vertebrates*.

The first vertebrates appeared in the Paleozoic. They are believed to be the descendants of animals similar to sea urchins and starfish; they were primitive fish.

Gradually — evolution always adds up to millions of years — the fins of some of these fish began to resemble legs.

Some of these fish with "legs" succeeded in leaving the water and crawling upon land. These amphibians in turn evolved into reptiles, which diversified later in an incredible fashion: dinosaurs, flying reptiles, marine reptiles...and later, birds and mammals.

The Human Was Still Far Away

The human was still millions of years away. However, a group of modest-looking reptiles appeared and evolved gradually into mammals. This is why they are called mammallike reptiles.

The first mammals had very unassuming looks. Like reptiles, however, they diversified enormously. We are particularly interested in one of the many lineages of mammals: insectivores, represented today by hedgehogs, moles and so forth.

Some insectivores were in fact the ancestors of primates. They resembled the present-day tree shrews of Southeast Asia. Only a small step led to the first lemurs, small animals with a pointed snout, such as

 Our Family of Primates

The class of mammals is divided into smaller groups (orders) that have common characteristics. Such is the case for the order of primates. Primates walk on the whole sole of the feet (they are called plantigrades). The fingers and toes have flat nails. They have all the types of teeth: incisors, canines, and molars. The eyes as well as the brain are very well developed. Most primates live in the forests of warm regions.
Among them are
— Prosimians: tree shrews, lemurs, and tarsiers
— Monkeys and apes
— Hominids: humans and our ancestors
We are the only primates that always walk upright that have adapted to all climates of the earth, from the equatorial jungles to the polar icecaps.

Archaeopteryx, the first "bird," *lived in the Mesozoic. Large as a pigeon, it probably glided from tree to tree. In fact, it had the wings and feathers of a bird and retained the claws and teeth of the reptiles from which it descended.*

the present makis of Madagascar. Lemurs are considered primates.

Thus appeared the order to which humans belong together with monkeys and apes. Human beings were, however, still far in the future.

Family Tree of Primates. *The dates are approximately those of the appearance of the various types of primates.*

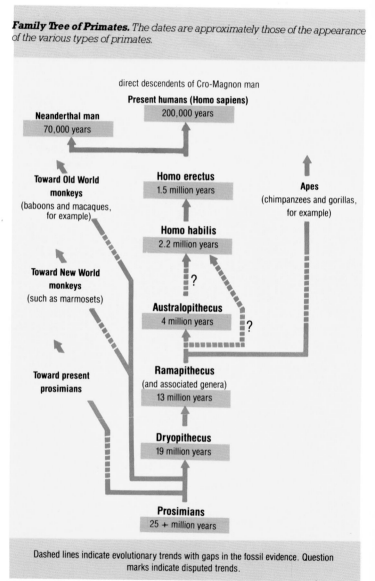

direct descendents of Cro-Magnon man

Present humans (Homo sapiens)
200,000 years

Neanderthal man
70,000 years

Toward Old World monkeys
(baboons and macaques, for example)

Homo erectus
1.5 million years

Apes
(chimpanzees and gorillas, for example)

Homo habilis
2.2 million years

Toward New World monkeys
(such as marmosets)

?

Australopithecus
4 million years

?

Toward present prosimians

Ramapithecus
(and associated genera)
13 million years

Dryopithecus
19 million years

Prosimians
25 + million years

Dashed lines indicate evolutionary trends with gaps in the fossil evidence. Question marks indicate disputed trends.

This Triconodon attacking a lizard is one of the oldest mammals. Mammals gradually spread over the entire earth.

What Is a Mammal?

The group (zoologists say the "class") of mammals differs from other animals by the fact that females provide milk for the young from the mammary glands—hence their name. The great majority of mammals live on land. However, some are aquatic: dolphins, whales, and other cetaceans. Some are half-aquatic, such as seals and sea lions. Some even fly: bats. Let us not forget that the human also is biologically a mammal.

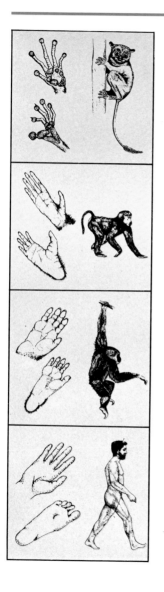

A Last Common Link

In the Tertiary, primates appeared that resembled and were the ancestors of present macaques or baboons. Some of these monkeys and apes evolved differently. They became taller and the brain developed. They gradually became anthropomorphs — that is, manlike monkeys or apes. They were the ancestors of the present apes: gibbons (with several species), orangutans, gorillas, and chimpanzees.

More precisely, one ancestor of large apes seems to have been *Dryopithecus*.

The Evolutionary Bush

Imagine evolution as a bush with many branches. From one twig—the primates— many little twigs branched out, each at different times and each leading eventually to different groups. One such twiglet, which led to the orangutans, separated from the main primate twig about

Tarsier, baboon, chimpanzee, and man: four stages in the evolution of the hand and the foot of primates.

The Toolmaker

It was formerly generally accepted that our main characteristic is the making of tools. Various animals use tools, however, in the wild and in the laboratory. For instance, chimpanzees strip the bark and leaves from tree branches, stick them in termite nests, take them out covered with termites, and lick them. It is more accurate to say that we are different from the other animals, even the other primates, in our consciousness, our awareness of ourselves, and in an ability for language. Humans, of course, knew how to cut flints and stones that they used for many purposes. This is why the discovery of cut stone implements at prehistoric sites indicates the past presence of humans.

16 million years ago. This was *Ramapithecus.*

At one time it was thought that *Ramapithecus* was an early hominid, but now it is known that it was not bipedal and shared many features with the orangutans. This kind of discussion is frequent among anthropologists. What is believed one day is often challenged by a new discovery made the next day.

Other groups, leading to gorillas and chimpanzees, branched off later. (The groups leading to the Old World monkeys and the gibbons had branched off earlier.) The group that led to human beings branched off latest of all, sometime between 5 and 8 million years ago.

All the primates and all the hominid species that are most closely related to the human, including *Homo sapiens,* our species, probably arose and developed in Africa and later spread to other continents. We believe this because it is in Africa that the oldest fossils and the oldest advanced stone tools are found.

A change of environment which was critical for the future of the human species: leaving the protective forests for the wide open spaces of the savanna.

From Lucy to the Neanderthal

Anthropologists rely on the the fossil record to provide information about early species. Unfortunately, from about 14 to about 4 million years ago, there is a gap. It is known that during that time, about 7.5 to 4.5 million years ago, there were major environmental changes in Africa. Perhaps these provided the push for the next development, because by 4 million years ago living beings appeared that were very close to us.

They were first discovered in South Africa and were considered to be monkeys or apes. Thus, they were called *Australopithecus* (*pithekos,* meaning monkey in Greek). In fact, they should rather have been called Australanthropus (from the Greek *anthropos,* meaning man). It is certain that some of them made tools. They walked upright, and their teeth were like ours. Therefore, we are dealing with humans, not apes.

These australopithecines lived not only in southern Africa but also in the eastern portion of that continent: Tanzania, Kenya, and Ethiopia. The discoveries made at the sites of the Olduvai Gorge in Tanzania and those at Omo and Afar in Ethiopia became famous.

A Touching Testimony

The discovery that was made a few years ago at Laetoli in Tanzania is particularly striking. It consists of the footprints of two australopithecines miraculously preserved for 3 million years. One set of footprints was appreciably larger than the other. The smaller ones stopped along their way, turned left before accelerating. Did the larger individual, an adult, scold the young?

The appearance of australopithecines has been reconstructed by their numerous fossil remains. They stood

Discoveries of fossil humans made the Omo valley in Ethiopia famous. Many other discoveries can be expected since tons of fossil bones are still buried in that valley.

A Famous Hoax

A very extraordinary human skull was found in 1908 in southern England. This Piltdown man excited most scientists. Was it filling the gap that remained in our knowledge of evolution? Was it the "missing link" between ape and human so eagerly searched for? Theories and controversies multiplied.

The truth was revealed in 1953. The skull was a hoax. A forger had put together the skull of a modern man with the jaw of an ape, with the teeth filed to disguise them.

Caught by a storm *these austrolapithecines built a shelter made of intertwined large logs and branches.*

almost upright and were 1.30 to 1.55 meters high (4.27 to 5.09 feet). The females were generally smaller than the males. The skull had a receding forehead (that is, inclined backward), massive brow ridges, and protrusive jaws (called prognathism). All these characteristics were still primitive but the biped position is a human characteristic, as is the nature of their teeth.

How Old Is Lucy?

There are three species of *Australopithecus*. The oldest is *Australopithecus afarensis*. This was also the smallest, only about 1.3 meters tall (just over 4 feet), and slender. The next was *Australopithecus africanus*, which was still small and relatively small-boned. The last, *Australopithecus robustus* (or *boisei*), was 1.55 meters tall (almost 5 feet) and heavier. As small as these hominids were, they were very strong.

Until Lucy, an *Australopithecus afarensis* female, was discovered in 1974 in the Afar depression in Ethiopia, it was thought that the oldest australopithecines were less than 3 million years old. Lucy, however, is known to be at least 3.5 and maybe almost 4 million years old.

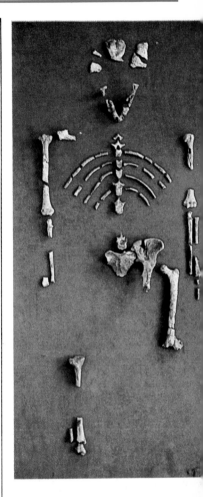

The skeleton of the famous Lucy, *named after a Beatles song the scientists were listening to while excavating and making the discovery.*

Life of the Australopithecines

Australopithecines lived in the African savanna. Some of them made tools out of quartz or basalt. They could be used for hunting: the prey may have been small animals, such as porcupines. Australopithecines might also have eaten carrion. They probably also ate insects and fruit and vegetables. They were omnivores.

The fauna of the African savannas at the time of the australopithecines included rather fearsome species—for instance, the saber-toothed tiger *(Machairodus)*, *Dinotherium,* a kind of elephant with downward pointed tusks, and *Dinopithecus,* a baboon the size of the gorilla.

The last australopithecines disappeared about 1 million years ago.

What Is a Species?

Look at a horse, Equus caballus. *It has four long legs ending in solid hooves. It has a tail, a long neck, a mane, ears that stick up from its head, and big teeth suitable for eating plants. It is a herbivore. Regardless of the pattern of its coat, its color, or the length of its tail, all horses display the same characteristics. These are transmitted to their young, which in turn, when adults, are passed on to their descendants. Therefore they are a group of similar individuals that are capable of interbreeding, and their offspring, which have the same attributes, are also capable of producing horses. This is a species.*

A windfall for Homo habilis! *A* Dinotherium *is dead and they cut up its carcass with tools.*

Homo habilis of Uncertain Origin

About 2 million years ago, long before the extinction of the australopithecines, a new species of hominids appeared: *Homo habilis*. It is the first species that anthropologists linked to the genus *Homo*, "man."

Indeed, this newcomer had a more developed brain than *Australopithecus*: the average was greater than 600 cubic centimeters (maximum 800) whereas in the latter the brain was 450 to 500 cubic centimeters.

Homo habilis, 1.50 meters high (almost 5 feet), svelte with a rounded skull, lived along the shores of the lakes of East Africa. Their tools were more sophisticated than those of the australopithecines, hence the designation "habilis" (able). It is thought that they threw crude polyhedral stones to kill their relatively small prey.

This is about all we know about them. Even their origins

Machairodus *ready to attack Hipparion, a distant relative of the horse.*

remain obscure. Some anthropologists think that they might have been simply a more evolved gracile australopithecine. Others are convinced that they belong to a new lineage of more human character.

At any rate, *Homo habilis* lived for a long time in East Africa together with robust australopithecines. From recovered bones, it is possible to say that the former preyed sometimes on the latter.

A New Step Toward the Modern Human

It is clear now that *Homo habilis* is the ancestor of a more evolved species: *Homo erectus*, or, in other words, the "man who stood upright." In fact, this designation is not quite fair because it could have applied to previous hominids.

Homo erectus is represented by several famous fossils: *Pithecanthropus* of Java, *Sinanthropus* of China, and the Heidelberg man. The human lineage was no longer limited to Africa.

Homo erectus measured 1.55 to 1.65 meters (just over 5 to 5.41 feet). The skeleton was quite similar to that of the modern human, but the skull preserved earlier characteristics: very protrusive jaws (prognathism), a receding forehead, and massive brow ridges. The cranial capacity ranged from 780 to 1225 cubic centimeters.

This species, which appeared, as mentioned before, 1.5 million years ago, became extinct about 150,000 to 250,000 years ago. Therefore, *Homo erectus* and their relatives *Homo habilis* lived at the same time as some australopithecines. Indeed, not every type of early hominid disappeared with the appearance of another. There were numerous overlaps.

The Discovery of Fire

Homo erectus had clearly better ways of living than australopithecines and *Homo habilis.* They made bifacial (two-sided) tools—that is, flints cut on both faces by means of a variable number of flakes. These bifacial tools represented two successive types of "industries": Abbevillian and Acheulian, named for two localities of northwestern France, Abbeville and Saint-Acheul, where the first specimens of these tools were found.

Furthermore, *Homo erectus* was the first to "discover" fire by striking two flints to produce a spark. This discovery occurred about 400,000 years ago and revolutionized the life of humankind. Indeed, by means of fire, *Homo erectus* could light their dwellings, cook their food, and warm themselves during the particulary rigorous winters of the glacial periods. They gathered around the hearth and developed social habits.

The Neanderthal: A Cousin

Evolution can be compared to a bush whose branches and numerous ramifications from a common trunk represent the diversification of species. (The name "family tree" has been given to such a representation, when applied to a human or animal family, which shows the lineage of descendants and

Boucher de Perthes

Around 1830, a custom officer, Jacques Boucher de Perthes, was digging in the gravels of the valley of the Somme near Abbeville in northwestern France. He discovered strange-looking flint pebbles. He understood that they were tools made by prehistoric people. Scientists of his time made fun of him because for them these pebbles were "games of nature." Boucher de Perthes persisted in his demonstration of the real nature of these flint pebbles and with him the study of prehistory was born.

When an excavation site is found, the long investigation of paleontologists and anthropologists begins: each bone and each object or fragment of object is cleaned and labeled. Notes, maps, and photographs are gathered in an attempt to reconstruct the life of prehistoric people.

the succession of generations issued from two ancestors.)

The family tree of the primates (page 18) shows the branch of *Homo erectus* giving rise to two distinct branches that strongly resemble each other. The first one is the Neanderthal and the second the Cro-Magnon, thought to be our direct ancestor.

The Neanderthal lived between about 100,000 years to 40,000 or 35,000 years ago.

The name came from the Neanderthal valley near Düsseldorf in West Germany where the remains of the first specimens were found in 1856.

The discovery consisted of a skullcap with archaic characters; it displayed a receding forehead and huge brow ridges. At the time, its appearance surprised many and its origin was questioned, and numerous hypotheses were presented.

Subsequently, numerous bones of the Neanderthal were discovered throughout Africa, Asia, and Europe. The most famous is the man from La Chapelle-aux-Saints (Corrèze, central France).

The Neanderthal man can be visualized as being about 1.6 meters high (5.25 feet), with an elongated skull, a prominent face, a robust jaw, and without a chin.

How Did they Live?

The ways of living of the Neanderthal shows a clear progression over those of *Pithecanthropus* and *Homo erectus*. Their industry has been called Mousterian from the village Le Moustier in Dordogne (southern France) where the first remains of this industry were found. They consist not only of bifacial tools but also of

Two Famous Examples of Homo erectus

In 1891, a Dutch physician, Eugène Dubois, extracted at Java the bones of Pithecanthropus. The discovery of this "man-like ape" (thus designated at that time) was a sensation.

The discovery made in 1921 of Sinanthropus in China became just as famous. Father Teilhard de Chardin studied it. Unfortunately, most of the bones of Sinanthropus disappeared during the war between China and Japan.

The discovery of fire was an important step in the history of our ancestors. These were the methods used to produce fire.

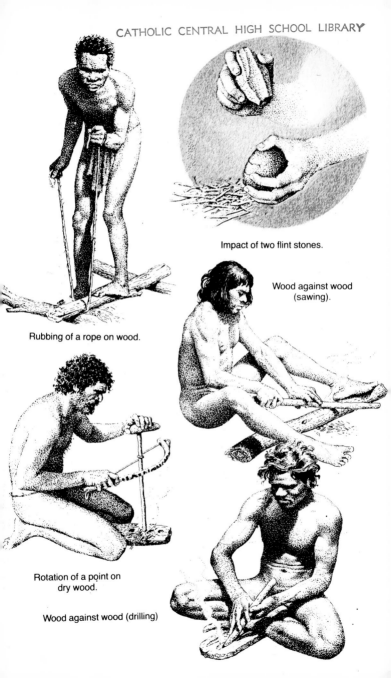

Impact of two flint stones.

Wood against wood (sawing).

Rubbing of a rope on wood.

Rotation of a point on dry wood.

Wood against wood (drilling)

points, nosed scrapers, and sidescrapers.

The first burials appeared mainly with the Neanderthal. At the Monte Circeo (Central Italy), bones of Neanderthal people were discovered, buried close to bodies of horses, hyenas, and elephants.

Another important step, language, may have begun with the Neanderthal. Indeed, it seems that they articulated almost as well as we do although their vocabulary was probably still rudimentary.

How was this evolution established? The organs that allowed our ancestors to change from shrieks to articulated language have obviously not been preserved. However, the curvature of the bones at the base of the skull is related to the capacity of speaking. Studies indicate that australopithecines were barely capable of babbling whereas the Neanderthal was capable of a true language.

A Lineage Without a Future?

The Neanderthal was thus not a heavy brute as is so often represented. They were really our cousins, almost our brothers and sisters.

They became extinct 40,000 to 35,000 years ago for yet unknown reasons. Were they the victims of a planetary epidemic? Or were they hunted, cornered, and finally massacred by a conquering species: ours? Indeed, their disappearance coincides with the appearance and development of new people: the Cro-Magnon, our direct ancestors—this time our real "fathers."

The view that the Neanderthal was a total side-branch of human evolution is today very widely accepted. Neanderthal is considered a variant of *Homo sapiens* physically adapted to the region and time period in which they were found.

What Fossils Do Not Show

Over a few tens of millions of years, an important evolution took place that led from Cenozoic primates to human beings.

It is quite well-known how this evolution changed the skeleton of the species that succeeded each other. However, it is not known when and

These Neanderthal people are burying their "old" (40 years) chief who has died. In order to cover the corpse with turf, they used the shoulder blades of bisons. Then, large stones were rolled over the tomb to protect it from hyenas.

Using a stone, our ancestors fractured another stone and then shaped the fragment to give it a sharp edge on one side.

The rock fragment is shaped on both faces to form a double-sided sharp object called a bifacial implement.

Later, techniques improved. Using a bone, humans extracted long sharp double-flaked fluted blades from flint rock.

how the nonpreserved organs were modified. Only inferences similar to the one made previously concerning language give some clues.

For instance, will it ever be known at what stage hominids lost their long, thick body hair?

Two Chromosomes Apart

The human lineage displayed a genetic evolution parallel to its anatomic one. The genetic evolution was not discovered by paleontologists but by biologists using microscopes. Genetics is the science that studies heredity—namely, the transmission of physical characteristics from parents to offspring among humankind as well as other animals and plants.

Sidescraper

Point

Bifacial implement

Tools of Neanderthal man.

Nosed scraper, 300,000 years old

Living beings consist of billions of cells. Each cell has a nucleus that contains thread-like bodies called chromosomes, which control heredity.

Each cell of modern anthropoid apes contains 48 chromosomes, whereas each cell of a human being has only 46. One can assume that the Cenozoic anthropoid apes also had cells with 48 chromosomes. Therefore, by means of a sequence of rather complicated processes, two chromosomes were lost during the evolution of humans.

This difference, although it seems of little importance, is nevertheless responsible for the unbridgeable gap between ape and human.

The orangutan of Borneo and Sumatra is a more distant relative of the human than the chimpanzee or the gorilla.

Hunters and Artists

The 4.5 billion men and women who today live on the earth differ in the color of their skin and their size, or by their mores and customs. Nevertheless, they all belong to the same species: Homo sapiens (often called Homo sapiens sapiens to distinguish it from Homo sapiens neanderthalensis, the Neanderthal). This designation does not mean "wise man," as sometimes believed, but "the one who knows," or, in other words, a human being that possesses the memory and intelligence necessary to study and try to understand the surrounding world. They also had language which served to transmit knowledge and to allow one human to learn from another.

Homo sapiens sapiens appeared about 35,000 years ago. They already had a modern anatomy. The skeleton is identical to ours. If a Homo sapiens of that time came back to us, he or she would appear perfectly ordinary.

Cro-Magnon

There are several types of fossil *Homo sapiens*, which are distinguished by small differences. The most famous is the Cro-Magnon. The name derives from the Cro-Magnon site near Les Eyzies in the Périgord in central France. At that location, during the construction of a railroad in 1868, the bones of five individuals were found in an overhanging rock shelter. Subsequently, other bones of the same type were discovered in other regions of France as well as in Germany, Belgium, Great Britain, and North Africa.

The Cro-Magnon was 1.8 to 2 meters tall (5.5 to 6.5 feet). They had a long skull and a high forehead.

Conquering the World

Did *Homo sapiens* appear at the same time in several places

With ocher, an iron ore with a color range from yellow to red, mixed with animal fat, this prehistoric artist sketches a bison on the wall of a cave.

On the ivory of this mammoth tusk found in Switzerland was delicately incised the figure of a reindeer. During the Pleistocene glaciations, reindeers and mammoths lived all over Europe.

on earth? Or, on the contrary, was the planet populated from a single "birthplace"? It is clear from the fossil evidence that *Homo sapiens* arose in Africa, as did all the hominids, and then rapidly spread across Asia, Europe, Australia, and the Americas.

Present evidence indicates that humans reached North America from Siberia about 30,00 years ago. At that time, the Bering Strait did not exist because sea level was lowered by the last glacial advance. Siberia was then connected to Alaska by a broad expanse of land. Therefore, migrating tribes could walk on dry land from one continent to the other. The ancestors of the earliest Americans were therefore of Asian origin.

From Alaska, they penetrated the rest of North Amer-

ica about 12,000 years ago when a corridor opened between the retreating ice sheet of Canada and glaciers on the Pacific Coast Ranges. Then, following the Isthmus of Panama, they reached South America, which they occupied as far south as Tierra del Fuego. These nomads started from the center of Asia and over generations completed an immense migration of about 20,00 kilometers (12,400 miles), half of the circumference of the world. This gradual colonization of the future New World began at the time of the Cro-Magnon and was only completed by 10,000 B.C.

Whether in America, in Europe, or in Asia, our ancestors had often to endure difficult living conditions, in particular frightful climatic variations. *Homo sapiens* had the intelligence and the physical capacities to confront them.

Confronting Glaciers

During the Quaternary, the northern regions of the earth were subjected four times to cold weather and associated glaciers. These were the glaciations. The last one occurred when the Neanderthal people and the first *Homo sapiens* coexisted. It started 75,000 years ago and ended between 10,000 and 9000 years before Christ.

The glaciers extended toward the south and covered mountains. They carved valleys. Sometimes, they were several hundred meters thick.

In order to escape the cold, people covered themselves with animal skins (bear, wolf, fox, lynx, and so on). Some took shelter in caves. When they were snowbound, they probably ate meat preserved by the cold.

They were also able to build artificial and partially subterranean shelters with skins stretched between posts. The Cro-Magnon, when the climate became warmer, built

These prehistoric javelin points with split bases were made from reindeer antlers.

such shelters in the open air. They also made dome-shaped huts using the bones of mammoths.

A Former Lord: the Mammoth

The mammoth was the most spectacular animal among the prehistoric fauna. It was like an elephant covered with a thick blond or reddish woolly fleece. It was, however, not exactly a giant in comparison with the dinosaurs that existed tens of million years earlier. It was only 3 meters (almost 10 feet) at the withers. However, the presence of two humps, one on the head and the other on the withers, gave it a strange look.

Its long curved tusks gave it an even more impressive look. These tusks were not always curved upward, as seen in many pictures, but often extended obliquely toward the front.

The mammoth is a well-known animal: frozen speci-

The Route Toward America

While chasing mammoths, the new Americans crossed on foot the land that connected what is now Siberia and Alaska. The route toward North America was open. The descendants of these people were to go as far as Tierra del Fuego. Glaciers locked the waters from the oceans and freed the straits, thus allowing the human migration.

nens have been discovered in the frozen muds (and not in ice) of Siberia. Their stomachs still contained plants which they had eaten: thyme, wild thyme, sage, and leaves of the birch tree. These plants are species that grow in the taiga or great northern forest. The mammoth was indeed an animal of the forest, not of the plain or tundra.

It should be noted, however, that in North America, mammoths with upward curved tusks lived in the plains. The first inhabitants of America hunted them. Furthermore, these Americans also hunted mastodonts, which were very similar to Siberian mammoths. Mastodonts disappeared about 10,000 B.C.

For prehistoric people, the mammoth was a very tempting "mountain of meat." However, it had to be captured. Hunters observed the trails taken by herds of mammoths crossing the forest. They dug a pit on one of these trails and then covered it with branches and turf.

Upon the arrival of a column of mammoths, the hunters went under cover on each side of the trail. As soon as the first mammoth fell into the pit, showers of arrows fell on it. Hunters also threw large rocks.

The other mammoths charged at hunters who fled through the tres or climbed up them. The wounded mammoth, losing its strength, became weaker and died. The hunters were unable to carry its corpse. Therefore, they cut it into enormous chunks of meat on the spot and then carried them on branches on their shoulders.

Our ancestors had to confront many other species of herbivores, today extinct—for instance, the woolly rhinoceros. This was a large rhinoceros with two horns on its snout: the longer front horn measured up to 1.5 meters (almost 5 feet). The woolly rhinoceros was covered by a thick black and reddish fleece. In the plains also ran troups of aurochs, those large wild oxes that survived in Asia and Europe until the Middle Ages.

Cave Beasts

Several large carnivores are classified as "cave beasts." However, the cave lion certainly lived in the steppes and the forests rather than in caves. It was a large, very supple feline with a slightly banded fur.

The cave bear also had very imposing looks. Upright, it reached 2.5 meters (over 8 feet). Its forelegs were very long so that its front body was elevated. It must have had an arched look with a slightly hanging head. Its snout was short.

Humans hunted it in various ways. Numerous traces of claws have been found on cave walls. It has been inferred that hunters placed traps or nets inside the caves in order to

Recognizable by its humps, by its long curved tusks, its thick woolly fleece, a mammoth is being carved in stone on a cave wall at Rouffignac, in Dordogne in central France.

capture the animal. Thereafter, they finished killing it with blows from clubs or stones as proven by the discovery of numerous fractured bear skulls.

People then ate the animal's meat, including the marrow of its bones, which are sometimes found broken for this purpose. Claws and teeth were used to make necklaces and the fur, of course, to provide body coverings.

An enormous cave hyena also existed, as tall as a lion and with a gray spotted fur. It may have prowled around dwellings scavenging for garbage.

Marvelous Cave Paintings

Mammoths, felines, aurochs, bisons, horses, reindeer, and other animals are the "heroes"

of splendid cave paintings that brought fame to many caves in France and in other countries. The oldest of these cave paintings date back some 25,000 years.

Started some 15,000 years ago and continued from generation to generation, the paintings at Lascaux (Dordogne) are the most famous: aurochs and horses are particularly well displayed there. In the same region are the caves of Font-de-Gaume and of Rouffignac. The latter is famous for its mammoths. In the Pyrenees, the caves of Niaux and Les Trois-Frères must be mentioned among many others. In Spain, the caves of Altamira have become world famous and equal to the one at Lascaux.

__This mammoth was sinking__ into a swamp. A godsend for these men who witnessed its agony. In the Siberian taiga, one of these mammoths may occasionally be found today preserved in frozen peat for thousands of years.

How did prehistoric people achieve such masterpieces? At first, they needed light. They hollowed out a rock and put there oil or fat, which they burned with a wick made from a plant substance.

To paint, they used various coloring materials: ocher, an iron ore, to obtain the yellow or red color; charcoal for the black; chalk for the white color; and so on. These materials had to be crushed into powder, which was then mixed with oil or water.

In order to decorate vaults or walls that were difficult to reach, they did not hesitate to construct scaffolds held together with ropes: a fragment of a scaffold was found at Lascaux.

Engravings, Sculptures, and Strange Objects

Prehistoric art also includes engravings and sculpture. The former were made with burins or chisels, the latter with pickaxes. In both cases, the rocks used were limestone or clay. Sometimes, artists simply

Another animal of the Ice Age, today extinct, was the woolly rhinoceros, which is sometimes portrayed on the walls of caves.

The Ossuary at Solutré

At Solutré (Saône-et-Loire, eastern France), a high cliff dominates the plain. At the foot of this cliff were found an extraordinary pile of bones of wild horses. All together, at least 10,000 horses had died there!

But how? Some experts believe that prehistoric hunters stampeded the horses, which panicked and jumped over the cliff. It is also possible that they fell accidentally from the top of the cliff: horses in the front of the herd saw the danger, but those following them did not know and simply continued to push forward.

carved with their fingers in clay.

Toward the end of prehistoric times, engravings became more and more delicate. In fact, the techniques used for these engravings and sculptures are still poorly known. Close to sculptured friezes were found pickaxes made from flint, which probably served as burins.

Bones and ivory were used very frequently by prehistoric people. They made shafts for daggers, flutes (after having pierced them with holes), and other objects. Or they made small statues of women with curved and voluptuous contours, which were nicknamed "Venus" by anthropologists. Reindeer antlers were made into harpoons, javelin points, or javelin throwers.

A javelin thrower has on one end an oval hole and on the other a hook. It is believed, but without certainty, that prehistoric hunters threw their javelins with these throwers—hence their name. At any rate, these throwers are among the most beautiful sculptured pieces of prehistoric times. On the side of the hook are often sculptures of animals—ibexes (wild goats) or grouse, for instance.

Oil lamp discovered at Lascaux: cut in sandstone, it is more than 15,000 years old.

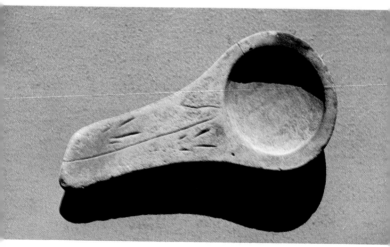

Also at Lascaux, *a splendid horse painted with ocher. The artists depicted its flight under a shower of arrows.*

 ### *The Discovery of Lascaux*

Robot did not return. On September 12, 1940, four boys were worried about a dog that had disappeared into a hole. Were they going to lose it like this during a walk in the countryside of Périgord, which had started so well?

In order to find the dog, the children crept into the hole. Robot was indeed there. And what it had "discovered" was fantastic. Under the light of a flashlight appeared splendid frescoes. The cave of Lascaux had just been discovered.

Perforated staffs seem even more enigmatic. They are also made from reindeer antlers and have a pierced hole, 3 or 4 centimeters in diameter (1 to 1.5 inches). There are sometimes two holes. These staffs are 15 to 30 centimeters long (5.85 to 11.7 inches) and show engravings of animals or enigmatic signs. They are considered, without any certainty, to be "bâtons de commandement" (commanding staffs) and to have been the scepters of tribal chiefs. Perhaps, though, they were made for other uses.

Strange Beings

Cave paintings remain, nevertheless, among the most beautiful art works of prehistoric times. The cave of Lascaux was nicknamed "the Sistine Chapel of Prehistory"—compared to the famous Vatican chapel with its numerous frescoes painted by Michelangelo in the sixteenth century.

A closer look at these frescoes shows some mysterious scenes. First, they represent a great number of mammals whereas birds are rare. Some screech owls and some bustards can be recognized. Furthermore, one sees at Lascaux a poorly identified bird sitting on a post. But that's it. Were hunters not interested in feathered game?

Representations of vegetables are essentially lacking, which seems strange. Furthermore, pictures of human beings are rare. Sometimes, one encounters strange beings, half-man, half-animal. For instance, in the cave of Combarelles (Dordogne) is a human body with the head of a

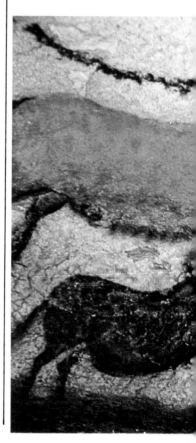

mammoth. Monstrous beings were engraved as well as sculpted. For instance, in the rock shelter of Roc (Charente, western France), a bison with the head of a wild boar was discovered. Elsewhere were found animals without heads.

On the whole, animals are nevertheless represented with

At Lascaux, *this aurochs and these horses were magnificently painted in many shades of ocher. The aurochs was the large wild ox of European prehistoric times. It was the direct ancestor of the bull of Camargue (southern France).*

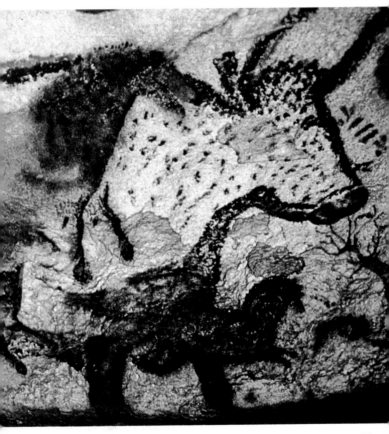

great accuracy. For instance, it is possible to identify the various species of large felines because of their whiskers, ears, mane (or absence of mane), goatee, and so on.

Why Such Masterpieces?

Why did prehistoric people produce such masterpieces? It was thought in the past that they painted these frescoes simply for the sake of art. This theory of art for art's sake has been abandoned. When people represented animals that they were hunting, they certainly hoped that they would be able to kill them later more easily. They probably were engaging in magic rituals similar to those of some present-day aborigines in Australia.

Indeed, some paintings show animals wounded or pierced by javelins. Some objects look like traps. People with animal heads might be wearing masks or other disguises in the attempt to approach animals more easily.

Representations of beasts might be explained in a similar fashion. These species may have been considered harmful and dangerous. Perhaps they were painted to facilitate their destruction.

It was probably also believed that sketching animals would increase their fertility and then they would be more abundant, so there

Mutilated Fingers

In the cave at Gargas (Haute-Garonne, southwestern France), cave paintings represent hands that often lack fingers. Why?

It is believed that mutilation was practiced among prehistoric peoples. During a sacrificial ceremony in the honor of a "Great Spirit," the fingers of a young man were cut. However, these amputations may have been caused more naturally by serious frostbite, which resulted in the loss of parts of the fingers.

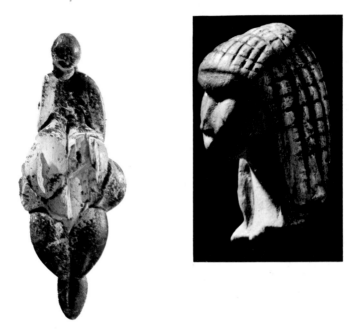

On the left: Prehistoric "Venus," *symbol of fertility.* ***On the right: Head of a*** ***woman,*** *sculpture on ivory from mammoth tusks. Discovered at Brassempoy (Les Landes, southwestern France) dating from 20,000 years ago.* ***On the bottom: Perforated staff*** *found in Dordogne in the cave of the Madeleine. Archaeologists do not know exactly the use of this object. Some believe that they were scepters, or "bâtons de commandement"; others think they were tent pegs.*

would be more to kill.

Some archaeologists go even further. According to them, some so-called primitive people believe that each tribe and each clan has an animal ancestor that remains its protector. This is called a totem. Therefore, some frescoes painted by our ancestors are alleged proofs of a totemic cult. This would explain among other things half-man, half-animal beings.

Each hypothesis probably has some particle of truth.

A Primitive Religion

Expressions of religion existed among early *Homo sapiens*.

Some traces even appeared earlier with the Neanderthal people.

The existence of burials containing gifts is very important. Indeed, people seemed to believe in an afterlife. Thus, at Grimaldi (Monaco) skeletons decorated with shells were found. Burials sometimes contained powdery ocher, which must have been sprinkled on the bodies.

Moreover, prehistoric people perhaps had magicians: in the cave of Les Trois-Frères exists the painting of a man covered with a skin and carrying the antlers of a reindeer. He was nicknamed the "sorcerer."

However, we know essen-

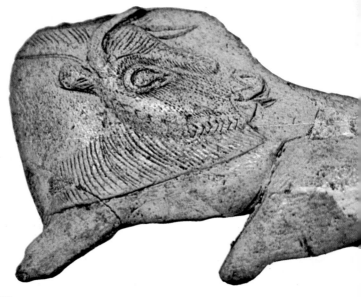

At Lascaux, a poorly understood picture, a "man-bird" points to a "post-bird," both sketched in a cartoon fashion.

Bison engraved on reindeer antler *found in the cave of Madeleine in the Dordogne.*

tially nothing about the religious beliefs and practices of our ancestors. Therefore, we are tempted to imagine them according to rites observed among the present "primitive" people, such as the aborigines of Australia or the Bushmen of Africa. However, there is no real evidence that they preserve untouched customs going back to prehistoric times.

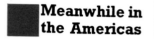

Meanwhile in the Americas

The history of primates in the New World is still very incomplete. Clearly, North America became too cold for primates during the Early Cenozoic (Tertiary). Even in South America, evolution did not go beyond the stage of monkeys and apes. In essence, the New World remained an immense open country until the Late Pleistocene when *Homo sap-*iens migrated from Asia through the Bering Strait which during a short span of time, including and following the last glacial advance, was the only route to the New World.

These first people appeared in North America between 25,000 and 15,000 years ago. They were nomadic hunters who lived mostly in western North America, in particular near ancient lakes. They made crude stone implements that were found together with the bones of extinct bisons, ele-

This strangely spotted horse, *with a human hand floating above it, can be seen in the cave of Pech-Merle (Lot, central France).*

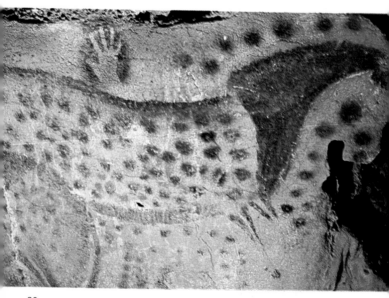

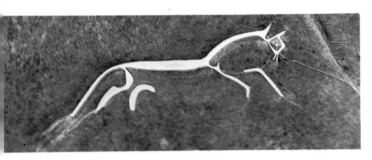

This white horse, engraved in the chalk of England, is 110 meters long (about 361 feet).

Neolithic statue found at Tripoljié, in Ukrania. It is a symbol of fertility of the earth.

phants, horses, camels, ground sloths, and various antelopes. There are traces of hearths and of human occupancy but no skeletons have been found.

Early migrations were followed by others: the Paleo-Indian hunting cultures had very characteristic stone implements consisting of several types of spears or arrow points with wide grooves or flutes on one or both sides. Their major sites were the plains east of the Rocky Mountains, such as at Folsom, New Mexico, where a particular type of fluted point called the Folsom point was found together with the bones of bisons. Other discoveries at Lindenmeier, Colorado, and Clovis, New Mexico, yielded a slightly older type of fluted point called the Clovis point and the bones of camel, bison, horse, musk ox, giant sloth,

61

and mammoth.

Nonfluted points, called Yuma points, were discovered nearby. The Folsom and Yuma techniques were probably in part contemporaneous, but the latter survived longer and became characteristic of subsequent human migrations. Again, at none of these sites, which are 12,500 to 7000 years old and occur mainly in the Great Plains from Canada to New Mexico, as well as east of the Mississippi, have human remains been found.

Caves in the Rocky Mountains yielded some important discoveries. At Sandia Cave, near Albuquerque, New Mexico, Folsom points were found above a layer containing older and cruder flaked points, called Sandia points, which are reminiscent of the Solutrean industry of Europe. In

These hands ornate the walls of a cave in Patagonia. The significance of this painting is not understood.

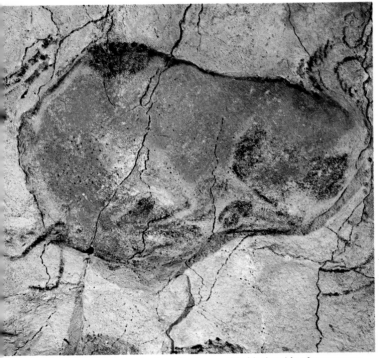

This bison painted in two shades of ocher and in black oxide of manganese
(on the right) is in the famous cave at Altamira, in Spain. Bisons lived in Europe
up to about 15,000 years ago.

the same layer were bones of
extinct species of wolf, jaguar,
ground sloth, horse, and tapir,
but again no human remains.
In the Folsom period, only one
human skull is known from a
site near Midland, Texas
(radiocarbon age, 12,000
years), as well as an almost
complete skeleton from the
site of Tepexpan, in the Valley
of Mexico, associated with
mammoth bones and fluted

implements. The estimated
age is 10,000 years.

Contemporaneous with the
hunting cultures in the plains,
early gathering cultures
existed in the intermontane
(between the mountains)
regions of the Rocky Mountains, where the vegetation, in
the relative absence of large
game, was extensively used
with related development of
grinding tools and basket mak-

63

ing. This was the Cochise Desert culture of Arizona and Utah, dated between 11,000 and 8000 years.

The oldest widely accepted evidence of human existence in South America (about 8600 years) comes from the Palliaike Cave, in southern Chile, where the burned bones of ground sloth, horse, and guanaco (a relative of the llama) were found together with human bones and stone implements. New evidence from South America shows that people were living in the Colombian highlands and Monte Verde in Chile about 13,000 years ago.

Subsequent human influxes, peoples who later developed cultures ranging from the Eskimo to the Inca, continued with the wider opening of the corridor between the retreating Canadian ice cap and glaciers of the Cascade Mountains, 10,000 years ago.

The glacially influenced moist and cool climate changed gradually to hot and dry in the Great Plains with the consequent extinction or migration of much of the Pleistocene fauna. Thus, the High Plains were abandoned by the hunting tribes, which moved into the eastern forest regions where they also gathered shellfish as indicated by numerous shell mounds found along river banks. The Desert Culture survived but began to be influenced by the beginning of agriculture, represented by the domestication of corn, beans, gourds, and squash, which started in the more favorable areas of Central America, particularly in Mexico. Indeed, excavations in the Tehuacán Valley, southeast of Mexico City, revealed a complete agricultural development 6000 to 5000 years ago. About 2000 years later, a refined and entirely agricultural society was thriving, which built cities, temples, and ceremonial grounds.

Meanwhile, the Eskimos developed their specialized society based on the hunting of sea mammals, whereas peoples, in the plains, while continuing to fish and hunt new game, moved out of the forests and deserts to settle and cultivate on the bottom lands along rivers. The reintroduction of the horse by the Spaniards in the sixteenth century led to the incorporation of the horse in the Plains cultures.

Now let us return to Europe where early archaeologic sites are much more abundant than in the Americas.

These strange "men-giraffes" are painted in a cave in South Africa.

From Prehistoric to Historic Times

After the last glaciation, about 9000 years B.C., some human groups gradually changed their ways of living. They lived no longer exclusively from hunting, fishing, and the gathering of wild plants. They discovered that the domestication of some animals and the cultivation of plants was possible. They thus slowly became farmers and animal breeders. Consequently, they abandoned their seminomadic ways of life and settled in villages. This is called the Neolithic Revolution (Neolithic being the later part of the "Old World Stone Age" or also the "Polished Stone Age").

The first domesticated animals, around 8000 years B.C., were the goat, the sheep, and the dog. The goat is a descendant of the ibex (wild goat) and the sheep of the mouflon (wild sheep). These two domestications occurred in the Middle East.

The dog was domesticated here and there in Europe from species derived probably from the wolf or the jackal. It may be assumed that wild "dogs" approached people on their own, helping them to capture prey. These "dogs" may be imagined, for instance, surrounding a herd of reindeers or of wild horses and putting them at the mercy of hunters. In appreciation, the latter may have given them some scraps.

Later, hunters or children may have brought home lost or

The shine of these sickles resulted from cutting grasses. This so-called cereal luster is due to the action on the cutting tools of minute abrasive siliceous bodies contained in the grasses.

Arrow head and ornaments found in a dolmen of the Aveyron (south-central France).

abandoned puppies. Thus, dogs gradually became integrated among humans to become watchdogs and, soon, sheepdogs.

Owing to domestication, people had soon at their ready disposal meat, leather, wool, milk, and other animal products.

Women Invent Agriculture

It is believed that women, who usually stayed more in the home region to care for the children, invented agriculture. Some among them must have noticed that seeds fallen on the ground began to germinate.

Thus, toward 6500 years B.C., wheat and barley were cultivated in the Middle East. Agriculture spread thereafter to southeast Europe and then to northern Europe. Vegetables—peas and beans—were also planted. Similarly, rice was planted in the Far East and corn and potatoes were cultivated in South America.

Many more human activities began at that time. People realized that clay fallen into fire becomes very hard and impervious to moisture. They thus had the idea to make pottery.

Pots were very useful to hold or transport water, for example. The invention of pottery led to the beginning of cooking as we know it.

They discovered that clay mixed with straw or other materials produced sturdier pottery.

At about the same time, people discovered weaving. They corded wool and then twisted fibers into threads. Linen, cotton, and silk were used later to make clothes, rugs, drapes, and other articles.

Basket making also began. Baskets, as well as mats—coarse materials used as rugs—were found very useful.

Some tools were then pol-

Tools and arm points dating from the first civilizations of the Metal Age.

ished. This is why the Neolithic Age was long called the "Polished Stone Age." This designation is not at all encompassing and is no longer accepted.

Menhirs and Dolmens: The Enigma of the Megaliths

The Neolithic Age is particularly famous for its megaliths ("large stones"), in particular dolmens and menhirs. They exist not only in Brittany but also in other regions of France (Aveyron and Ardèche), as well as in Great Britain, Scandinavia, and North Africa.

Menhirs were placed vertically in the ground. Some of them weigh up to 200 or even 300 tons. At Carnac (Morbihan, Brittany), menhirs form alignments 4 kilometers long (2.5 miles). Sometimes, as at Stonehenge in England, they are arranged in circles.

Dolmens are often shown in the form of a horizontal stone

Dolmen of Corbertella *(Catalonia, Spain). The covering slab weighs no less than 19 tons!*

Installation of a menhir: *hundreds of workers were needed to drag it on logs, hoist it up on a ramp, and drop it into a trench.*

supported by two vertical stones. However, some of them are much more complicated. They represent collective burials, often including a chamber with a passage leading to it. Dolmens are sometimes part of a cairn, that is, a mound of earth and stones covered by earth.

In southern England there is an impressive group of megaliths: Stonehenge. It was built between 1800 and 1400 B.C. by successive groups of people.

Stonehenge, when it was complete, was like a circle of megaliths, some 30 meters in diameter (98.35 feet), in the center of which stood five pairs of stones each one weighing 45 tons.

It was noticed that the main axis of the Stonehenge monument is oriented in the direction of the sunrise during the summer solstice, that is, where the sun reaches the highest position in the sky in the northern hemisphere (June 21 or 22 depending upon the year). Was this site built to worship the sun or to trace its course in the sky?

It is certain that Neolithic people had some knowledge of astronomy. It is possible that the megaliths at Carnac formed a moon observatory. This appears possible if one examines a map of the location of Carnac. When joining the menhirs and other megaliths by lines, directions are obtained that point to the sites of the rising and setting of the moon during its extreme phases (new moon and last quarter).

True Villages

The development of agriculture contributed, as mentioned, to the settlement of people. In Europe, people began to build wooden houses. In order to do that they had to cut trees with stone axes. Forests were reclaimed for cultivation. In the Middle East, houses were built with bricks made from mud.

In these first villages soon appeared the first shops—for instance, jewelers. Each village chose its chief who had to settle disputes and coordinate defense movements in case of war.

Discovery of Metals

The discovery of metals was a very important step in the history of humankind. People began to collect the ore found in river deposits (alluvium). Later, they excavated it from open pits, and finally from underground mines. Thus, copper was extracted in Spain, Austria, and Cyprus and tin mines were operated in Cornwall (England).

The age following the Neo-

View from the air of the alignments at Carnac, which remain puzzling. Was it an observatory?

lithic was therefore called the "Age of Metals," or Protohistory. It was divided successively into the Copper Age, the Bronze Age, and the Iron Age.

People learned about the smelting of metals in furnaces. They obtained alloys. Thus, they made axes, daggers, swords, bracelets, sickles, knives, halberts, and other metal objects.

Glass and Salt

It is not known exactly where and when how to make glass was discovered. We know for certain that beads of colored glass were found in burials in Italy and Austria.

At the end of the Bronze Age, salt mines at Hallstatt, in Austria, were actively exploited. Shafts went down to 250 meters depth (over 9800 feet). On the shores of Brittany and Normandy, salt was extracted from seawater.

History Began with Writing

It should be mentioned that the progress of civilization varied from one region to another. Therefore, it is difficult to establish a precise chronology. For instance, the pyramids of Egypt are older than the European megaliths.

The English village of Windmill Hill, (near Stonehenge), enclosed by ditches interrupted by causeways for the passage of the inhabitants.

Did Lake Dwellings Exist?

We have all seen representations of lake dwellings, that is villages built on piles on the shores of lakes. Such villages were located in or on Swiss Lakes.

Some experts believe that at the time these villages existed, they were not built in water because hearths and ashes were found by divers between piles. Perhaps these villages were built above ground level for protection against wild animals and raiding war parties.

In Mesopotamia, the first cities were built; they were true "city-states" dominated by high "tower-temples." The first people of Western Civilization were thus born in the Middle East and in the valley of the Indus.

Eventually, people invented writing. The development of the written word marked the end of prehistory and the beginning of history.

One of the earliest known examples of writing —seen on a Sumerian tablet.

Index

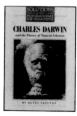